Healthy Sexuality

Kristen Kemp

Franklin Watts
A Division of Scholastic Inc.
New York • Toronto • London • Auckland • Sydney
Mexico City • New Delhi • Hong Kong
Danbury, Connecticut

Dedication

*To my mom, who bravely and patiently helped me
make it through puberty and everything else.*

Cover design by John Gibson.
Interior design by Kathleen Santini.
Illustrations by Leonard Morgan.

Library of Congress Cataloging-in-Publication Data

Kemp, Kristen.
    Healthy sexuality / Kristen Kemp.
        p. cm. — (Life balance)
Summary: Discusses aspects of sexuality, including gender characteristics, changing emotions during puberty, birth control, and sexually transmitted diseases.
Includes bibliographical references and index.
    ISBN 0-531-12336-7 (lib. bdg.)   0-531-16689-9 (pbk.)
    1. Sex instruction for children. [1. Sex instruction for children.]
I. Title. II. Series.
    HQ53.K45 2004
    613.9'071—dc22

                                    2003019771

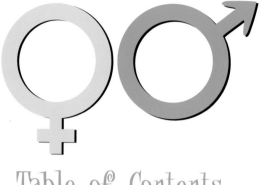

Table of Contents

Mastering Puberty

Growing up can't happen fast enough. Soon you'll get an extended curfew, your driver's license, and maybe even your first job. Every year, it seems, you acquire a little more freedom—finally. Along with these perks, though, you might notice a lot of weird stuff going on in your body. You see new hair in strange places, along with some big changes down below. But don't worry, things aren't as bad as they may seem. It only proves you're that much closer to young adulthood.

Everyone on the planet has experienced (or will) the emotional and physical challenges of growing up. Don't worry—it's all worth it in the end. Thousands—make that millions, even billions—of people around the world would agree.

Going through puberty and understanding male and female sexuality doesn't have to be a huge, scary ordeal. After reading this book, you'll feel far more comfortable with sex, puberty, body parts, and everything else you may have giggled at before. Any time you start to get embarrassed, just think of the kid sitting next to you in class. Whether or not you know his or her name, religion, or favorite TV show, you do know this for sure: He or she is going through the same sort of changes you are.

Mastering puberty is like learning to drive a car. You learn as you go. Before long, going through puberty will be as natural as pressing the gas pedal is for an experienced driver. And by the time *you're* driving, you'll be shocked to find that puberty is almost over, you survived, and the whole thing sped right on by.

One

All About Girls

"Weird hairs sprouted up on my body. Then my breasts started feeling sore. I got my period around this time, too. Sometimes I'm glad all of this has happened—I've looked forward to it my whole life. But there are also times when I just feel embarrassed and confused."
—Lacy, 14

You can't control what your body does, or the feelings that go along with it. Puberty is sometimes exciting (you're older!) and sometimes devastating (you just want to be a kid again!). Just so you know, all of your thoughts are healthy and wonderful and confusing. Once you understand *exactly* what's going on, you'll worry less.

Female Anatomy

Most women cannot point out and name the private parts of their own bodies. It's true! Maybe they don't take the time to learn, or they don't remember what they were taught in school. At any age, it can be embarrassing to ask a teacher, a doctor, or anyone else to explain this stuff. So keep reading, and you'll be armed with information that puts you ahead of many adults.

Am I Normal?

"All of a sudden I'm having dreams about boys, my body is changing shape, and I have to use deodorant. These things make me feel weird and embarrassed and sometimes even bad. Am I normal?" —Sasha, 12

It's totally normal to ask if you're normal. The thing is, everyone grows and develops at his or her own pace. So let's just ban the word normal right now. Nothing about your budding body is weird or strange, and your new feelings aren't anything to be embarrassed about. Chances are good that most people your age have the same concerns you do. That's not to say you won't get weirded out sometimes—we all do. It's, well... normal!

Sure, you may have a vague idea on vagina basics. But getting familiar with the proper terms will make you feel more comfortable about your body and the changes it is going through. Pay close attention to the pictures as well as the definitions on the next few pages. It's also a good idea to examine yourself using a hand mirror to make sure you understand everything. (Really!)

It's a good idea to examine yourself using a hand mirror to make sure you understand everything.

External Female Genitalia

vulva—This is the entire outer area of the female genitals. It basically includes everything you can see. Our culture puts a lot of emphasis on the vagina, which is inside the female body. *Vulva* is the correct term to use when you're talking about the general area or anything that happens outside the vaginal canal.

mons pubis—This is the soft pad of tissue where coarse, curly pubic hair grows. The tissue tends to get slightly rounder and thicker when puberty begins.

labia majora—These are the two larger folds of skin you see when your legs are closed. They protect and conceal the delicate tissue located just inside.

labia minora—When the labia majora are spread open, you can see these two smaller lips located just inside. They are made of very delicate tissue that contains blood vessels and oil glands. Kind of like the tissue just inside your nose, the labia minora are meant to stay slightly lubricated at all times.

clitoral hood—This small fold of skin lies just above the crease in the labia majora. (You may have to part the lips just a little bit to see it.) It covers and protects the clitoris from irritation and constant stimulation.

Female Anatomy

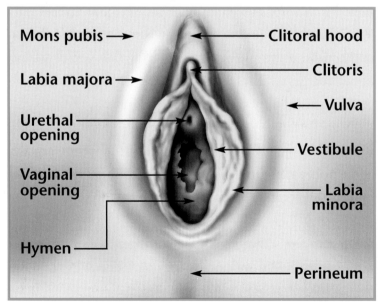

Mons pubis →   ← Clitoral hood

Labia majora →   ← Clitoris

   ← Vulva

Urethal opening —

   ← Vestibule

Vaginal opening —

   ← Labia minora

Hymen —

   ← Perineum

clitoris—The pea-size clitoris is the only organ in the body whose sole purpose is to make its owner feel good. It is a nerve-rich area that fills with blood during sexual arousal (when one becomes sexually excited), causing pleasurable sensations. Tiny oil glands surround it, giving it a slightly shiny appearance. Some girls have a visible clitoris; for others, it's tucked under the clitoral hood until they become sexually aroused.

vestibule—This is the sensitive patch of skin just inside the labia minora and surrounding the opening of the vagina.

urethral opening—Between the clitoris and the vagina opening is this tiny hole that allows urine to leave the body. The size and the shape of the opening vary greatly among girls.

vaginal opening—This is the skin just outside the vaginal canal. Don't think of the opening as a hole. It's usually open just enough to allow vaginal discharge and menstrual blood to flow out. It stretches greatly during sexual intercourse (when a penis is inserted into the vagina) and childbirth.

hymen—Located just outside the vaginal opening, the hymen is a thin ring of tissue. The tissue can expand and even tear ("break") during tampon insertion or vigorous activity such as horseback riding. Sometimes it doesn't tear until you have sex for the first time.

perineum—This smooth patch of skin lies just below the vaginal opening. It extends to the anus. Sometimes it is hairless; other girls may have pubic hair on the perineum.

anus—The opening of the rectum, it allows waste to pass through the body as a bowel movement.

Internal Female Reproductive Organs

vagina—This is the canal that leads from the opening of the vulva to the cervix of the uterus. The interior lining is a mucous membrane (kind of like the inside of your nose), and its two walls are made of muscular tissue. The muscles stretch to accommodate sexual intercourse and giving birth. The vagina is also the passage for menstrual and other discharges.

cervix—This muscular structure at the end of the vaginal canal serves as the neck of the uterus (see definition p. 13). It has a dimple at the end that has a microscopic opening that allows sperm through for fertilization. The opening also expands wide enough during childbirth for a baby to pass through.

Female Reproductive Organs

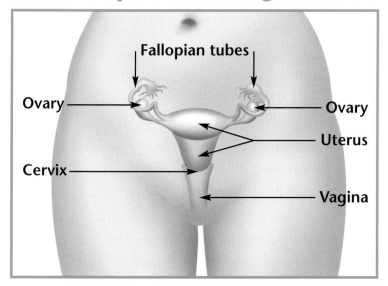

Fallopian tubes

Ovary

Ovary

Uterus

Cervix

Vagina

uterus—Just above the cervix lies the uterus, a small, muscular, pear-shape organ that holds a baby during pregnancy. It is usually slimmer than your finger, but it expands to accommodate a baby, then retracts after birth. The uterus builds and sheds its lining (called endometrial tissue) approximately once a month during the menstrual cycle (more on that later!).

Fallopian tubes—Extending out from the top of the uterus are a narrow pair of ducts. Called the Fallopian tubes, these ducts transport eggs from the ovaries (see definition p. 14) to the uterus.

ovaries—The ovaries are home to a woman's eggs. About once a month, an egg is released from an ovary and travels down one of the Fallopian tubes to the uterus. If the egg is fertilized, a pregnancy occurs. Without fertilization, the cycle of menstruation begins, meaning you will get your period.

Changes: When to Expect What

"My best friend started wearing a bra in the fifth grade. Now eighth grade is almost over, and I still don't have anything up there. How can this happen?"—Michelle, 13

Puberty tries your patience, there's no doubt about that. Luckily, while the changes (or lack thereof) are annoying, you can usually bet that your development is moving along at a pace that's healthy for you. A girl's physical development is usually based on heredity. To get a good idea of what's going to happen to you, ask your mom or older sister some personal questions. Find out when they first started wearing deodorant and a bra. Ask when they got their periods. Expect similar timing for you, especially if you share the same body type.

No one knows exactly why girls have different experiences. Researchers do know that puberty is starting younger. For example, in 1900 girls started their periods at an average age of 14. Today the age is 12. This could be because kids have access to more nutritious foods today. Ethnicity also

*To get a good idea of what's going to hap-
pen to you, ask your mom or older sister
some personal questions. Find out when
they first started wearing deodorant and
a bra. Ask when they got their periods.*

has something to do with it. One recent study showed that
half of African American girls began puberty by age eight.
Meanwhile only fifteen percent of Caucasian girls began
physically changing by that age. Experts are still trying to
figure out why.

To make puberty easier to track, British doctor J. M. Tanner
divided the process into the following five stages:

Stage 1
Ages 8–11—Ovaries begin to enlarge and make the hormone estrogen. At this point, you probably won't notice anything on the outside.
Stage 2
Ages 8–14—Estrogen levels increase in the bloodstream. Breasts form little buds, and the nipples stick out more, which may cause tenderness in the area. The body begins growing quickly; the hips broaden. Thin, fine, straight hair sprouts under arms and in the genital region.

Stage 3
Ages 9–15—The chemistry of the vaginal secretions becomes more like that of adults, and the vulva may look bigger. Breasts grow, and so does the area around the nipples called the areola. Height and weight increase while pubic hair gets darker. Menstruation is likely to begin.
Stage 4
Ages 10–16—Ovaries begin to become adult size. On the outside, the nipple and the areola form separate mounds. The body continues growing, and pubic hair gets thicker. If you didn't start your period in Stage 3, you probably will in Stage 4.
Stage 5
Ages 12–19—Ovaries become fully mature, and menstruation becomes more regular. Breasts become fully developed (meaning they'll probably stop growing). You reach adult height, too, though some girls still grow another inch or two.

Menstrual Cycles and Pregnancy

When we reach a certain age—during puberty—females are able to have a child. Once you first get your period, you'll have reached this amazing point in your life. Obviously you won't want to have babies for many years, but the way your body prepares for it every month is pretty darned cool.

The entire menstrual cycle usually lasts about twenty-eight to thirty days. On day one, hormone levels in the body are low, and the bleeding begins, lasting for about five days. After day five or so of your cycle, when the blood stops, the hormone levels begin to rise, telling the lining of the uterus (called the endometrium) to thicken and grow. This lining contains lots of minerals and vitamins; it is building up just in case the woman's body needs to nourish an egg and support a pregnancy.

Around day fourteen, her ovaries receive the signal that it's okay to release an egg into the Fallopian tubes. The ovaries usually release one egg each month; this is called ovulation. The egg travels down the tube for two days and is deposited into the uterus. Meanwhile the lining continues to thicken. This goes on until about day twenty-eight. At this point, if the egg has not been fertilized by a sperm, hormone levels that were slowly on the rise all month suddenly drop, and the uterus will begin to shed its lining. The woman sees it as menstrual blood, which is the first day of the next menstrual cycle.

In order to get pregnant, fertilization must occur. This happens when sperm comes into contact with the egg-in-waiting. The sperm and the egg meet during sexual intercourse, when the penis is inserted into the vagina. Adults who are trying to have a baby usually have sex during ovulation, which is when the egg is in the best position to become fertilized. If fertilization occurs, the egg plants itself in the uterine lining where it matures into a baby. At this point the woman stops getting her period.

> ### *Pregnancy* Before *Menstruation*
> *It's important to realize that you can get pregnant before the onset of your period, although this is rare. If a girl happens to have sexual intercourse right when the egg is released, fertilization can occur. While most girls will prefer to wait several years, it's important to understand that pregnancy is possible before menstruation starts.*

Period Products

During the past few hundred years, everything from rags and belts to rudimentary tampons made of wool have been used to control the flow of menstruation. Good thing for us, modern times mean better options.

Don't worry too much about where you'll be when you get your first period. Between the ages of eight and sixteen, all you can do is be prepared. The first period isn't very heavy for most girls. Instead of blood, you'll probably feel a little more wetness than usual. When you go to the bathroom, you'll see small reddish brown spots. You can probably stuff a few pieces of toilet paper into your underwear while you search for a maxi pad. Keep a pad and a spare pair of panties hidden away in your locker just in case it happens at school, or put a mini pad in your backpack or purse.

Pads

Pads, also known as sanitary napkins, are worn outside the body. The sticky side attaches to the inside of your underwear. The other side, which goes against your skin, is made of a soft, absorbent material that soaks up menstrual blood. Pads shouldn't be worn for more than four hours during the day or for eight hours overnight. Change them often to avoid odor. They cannot be flushed, so it's best to wrap them up in tissue or the wrapper they came in before throwing them away. You may also want to buy mini pads to use at the end of your period, when the flow is light.

Tampons

Tampons are worn inside your body. They look like a tube the size of your pointer finger with a string hanging down. The absorbent, cottonlike core is usually covered in plastic or cardboard. This part is called the applicator, and it helps you insert the tampon.

Tampons are safe to use from your very first period. You can wear one for up to four hours during the day, and it's fine to wear one overnight as long as you take it out in the morning. Read the directions on the box; some tampons are flushable, and others need to be thrown away in a garbage can. They come in different sizes and absorbencies, from slender to super. Start with slender, then buy bigger ones if necessary.

Tampon Tips

- *Tampons are easiest to use when your flow is heavy. You may find inserting them more comfortable then.*
- *If you have trouble inserting a tampon, put a bit of water-based vaginal lubricant such as K-Y Jelly on the rounded end of the applicator. A dab of Crisco also works (but use a new tub!). Don't use petroleum jelly (Vaseline) or lotions.*
- *When a tampon is inserted correctly, you cannot feel it. If it's uncomfortable, it's probably not in deep enough. Take out the tampon and try again.*
- *Unless you're asleep, always remove your tampon at least every four hours to avoid infections.*
- *Remember—tampons do not take away your virginity; that is a myth! They also can't get "lost" inside your body. Your cervix is a barrier that keeps the tampon in the vaginal canal (what goes in must come back out!).*

Is Something Wrong?

Once you have your first period, you may think—boom—you're going to have one every twenty-eight days for, like, ever. It isn't quite so calculated. Look at it this way: It takes lots of practice for you to learn to solve algebra equations. Your body needs practice menstruating much the same way. When you've just started, your hormones are still out of whack. It will probably take a few years for your body to get everything regulated. For the first year especially, it's common and healthy to have one period, skip one or two, then find yourself spotting before the next one. If you aren't on a schedule within a year and a half, you may want to talk to your doctor. Skipping your periods too often could be a sign of dangerous weight loss or other problems.

Breast Basics

No two breasts are quite the same—not even on one girl! So it's difficult to say exactly when you'll grow your breasts and how big they will get. Experts do know that just about all girls start growing them between the ages of eight and seventeen, and they take four to five years to fully develop. Heredity is the only thing that will determine your size—any pill, product, or exercise that promises to increase your bust is not going to work (some are even dangerous). Of course, if you gain a lot of weight at any time in your life, your breasts may get bigger. The opposite is also true—lose pounds and they might shrink.

The purpose of a woman's breasts is to produce milk to feed her baby. Of course, women today can choose if they want to breast-feed or buy baby formula at the supermarket. Biologically, though, that is the breasts' function. The breasts are made up of fat, glands, milk ducts, nerves, veins, arteries, and lymph nodes. The only muscles in the area are the pectorals, which are located underneath the breast tissue.

On the top of the breast is the nipple, which is in the center of the darker tissue surrounding it, called the areola. Nipples and areolae are different for every woman. Some women have larger ones, others have small ones. Fair-skinned girls will have pink nipples and areolae and darker-skinned girls may see brown tones.

When breasts begin to grow, they may seem sore when you lift your arms or turn over in bed. This is because your tissues are being stretched faster than your body can make new cells to keep up. Next thing you know, you feel like you have two big bruises. That feeling will go away within a few months. You may notice, however, that your breasts get sore before each period. This happens because your body is retaining fluid—stretching the nerves in the breasts and making them tender. Take acetaminophen (Tylenol®) or ibuprofen (Advil®) for relief.

Two

All About Boys

"I am so tired of having to place textbooks in front of my crotch during the most embarrassing times—like when I'm walking down the hallway at school. When will this end?"
—Ian, 12

Girls don't have a monopoly on body changes. Guys have important issues to deal with, too. But while girls are likely to talk to someone, such as their best friend or older sister, about such changes, boys tend to keep things bottled up. (Maybe that's why studies have shown that women are far more likely to go to the doctor than men are.) You still need advice, even if you don't ask for it.

You may know many of the schoolyard terms for male anatomy, so we'll stick to the medical ones. If you understand your specific body parts and the jobs they do, you'll feel more confident about yourself—especially when puberty really kicks in. So go through the definitions below, paying close attention to the diagrams. It's also a good idea to get a mirror and check yourself out. (You don't have to tell anyone!)

External Male Genitalia

penis—The male reproductive organ is made of spongy tissue and blood vessels. It fills with blood during sexual excitement, which causes an erection. Urine and semen both exit the body through the penis.

glans—Located at the tip of the penis, the glans is sometimes called the head. Because it is filled with nerve endings, it is pleasurable for the glans to be touched.

foreskin—All males are born with this thin layer of skin that covers and protects the glans of the penis. In the United States it is customary for the foreskin to be removed at the hospital shortly after birth, a process called circumcision. Jewish males are circumcised for religious reasons. Recently, though, more parents are choosing *not* to remove the foreskin, which is the custom in most of Europe. Either choice is healthy. Though circumcised and uncircumcised penises look slightly different, they function in exactly the same way.

urethral opening—This tiny hole at the end of the glans allows urine and semen to exit the body.

Male Anatomy

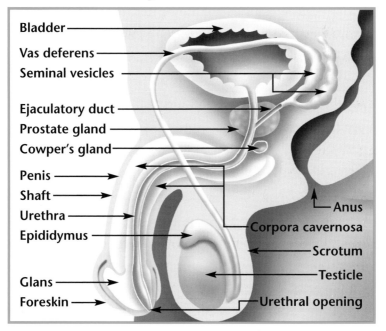

Bladder
Vas deferens
Seminal vesicles
Ejaculatory duct
Prostate gland
Cowper's gland
Penis
Shaft
Urethra
Epididymus
Glans
Foreskin
Anus
Corpora cavernosa
Scrotum
Testicle
Urethral opening

shaft—This is the long part of the penis, which contains muscle and erectile tissue. There is a lot of empty space in the shaft, which fills with blood during sexual arousal.

scrotum—This is the wrinkly sac of skin, divided into two parts, that holds and protects the testicles. The sac hangs outside the body, in the groin area between the legs. During puberty, hair begins growing on the scrotum.

testicles—These ball-shaped organs are inside the scrotum. They are also called testes (and are commonly referred to as "balls"). The testicles are the centers for sperm cells and testosterone production. When they begin to make testosterone, a male hormone, puberty begins.

anus—This opening between the buttocks allows waste to leave the body.

Internal Male Reproductive Organs

epididymis—This is a long, tightly coiled canal that lies within the scrotum and adjoins each testicle. It stores newly generated sperm. (If the coil were unwound, it would be twenty feet long!) This is the first stop for mature sperm on their way out of the body.

vas deferens—A continuation of the epididymis, this tube also transports sperm. The vans deferens extends from the scrotum to the abdominal cavity. It passes beind the bladder and joins the seminal vesicles.

seminal vesicles—These small, bulb-shaped pouches are located just outside the prostate gland. They produce some of the seminal fluid, which is part of semen.

ejaculatory duct—A short tube just above the prostate gland, this is where the vas deferens and the seminal vesicles connect. It transports sperm through the prostate gland and into the urethra.

prostate gland—This one-inch gland lies against the bottom part of the bladder. It secretes much of the seminal fluid. When combined with the other fluids in the seminal vesicles, the fluid carries sperm out of the body. The prostate gland grows bigger during puberty.

Cowper's glands (also called bulbourethral glands)—These are two pea-size bulbs, one on each side of the urethra. They produce a clear, sticky fluid that leaves the body just before semen does.

urethra—A tubelike vessel that runs through the shaft of the penis. It carries urine and semen, moving fluids from the bladder or the testicles to the urethral opening so that they can pass out of the body.

corpora cavernosa—Located inside the shaft of the penis, this is the spongy tissue that fills up with blood during sexual arousal.

sperm—Sperm aren't really organs, but they *are* cells on the inside of a boy's body. Sperm is the male sex cell. After puberty, males start producing sperm cells in their testicles. During sexual intercourse, these sperm sometimes join with female eggs to make babies.

Physical Development: When to Expect What

So you wanna be a man? Just sit back and let your body take care of everything! From the ages of nine to fourteen, boys start to mature in ways that will surprise even them. They don't have to worry about getting their period, of course, but guys have to deal with spontaneous erections, voice changes, growing genitals, and hair sprouting everywhere.

Why does puberty begin between the ages of nine and fourteen? Because the brain says so. The hypothalamus, pituitary, and pineal glands in your head send a signal down to the testicles. They get the message to begin making testosterone, a hormone that is more abundant in males than in females. That's when things really start to change. The testicles make sperm for the first time, and they aren't lazy—they produce between one hundred million to two hundred million sperm each day (most die in a natural process).

Meanwhile the testicles grow, and the scrotum that holds them hangs a little lower. Nature is brilliant—the scrotum hangs down and away from the body for a reason. Sperm that

Guys have to deal with spontaneous erections, voice changes, growing genitals, and hair sprouting everywhere.

are inside the testicles can't live at body temperature; they thrive in a slightly cooler environment. So the scrotum keeps them just outside the body where it's not too hot and not too cold. When a boy is cold, like in a freezing shower, his scrotum pulls the testicles in closer to his body where it's warm. If he's hot, the scrotum will hang down a little lower.

Along with producing sperm, a boy grows in height, hair begins to grow in his genital area, his penis gets longer, hair spurts out on his upper lip, and his voice deepens. It doesn't always happen in perfect order. One boy may stay the same height until the eighth grade while his friends tower over him. Then he'll shoot up all at once over a single summer. It's difficult to predict when each change will happen, but the chart below, by Dr. J. M. Tanner, can give you a general idea:

Stage 1
Ages 9–12—Testicles start churning out testosterone, but the boy can't tell. The only sign he'll have that puberty is beginning is probably a rapid growth spurt. He won't yet have hair or genital changes.

Stage 2

Ages 9–15—Muscles begin to develop and get stronger, especially in the chest and shoulders. The scrotum and the testicles finally get their growth spurt too. Thin, fine pubic hair may sprout at the base of the penis, and the area surrounding the nipple (called the areola) will darken.

Stage 3

Ages 11–16—The scrotum and the testicles continue to grow, and the penis starts to lengthen. Shoulders get broad, and more muscles develop all over the body. The pubic hair gets darker and coarser around the genitals. The very beginnings of a mustache may appear. The larynx also begins to grow, and that makes his voice deeper.

Stage 4

Ages 11–17—As sperm production kicks into gear, the first ejaculation (a release of semen) will take place. The penis not only gets longer but it also gets wider. Underarm and facial hair crop up, and the skin gets a little oilier.

Stage 5

Ages 14–18—Now he's really starting to look like an adult. Everything is pretty much in place during these years, but he may see more hair appear on his face and his chest.

Penises 101

We know that sperm are produced in the testicles, but how the heck do they make their way out of the penis? Here's the long story made short: After the sperm are produced, they travel from the testicles to the surrounding tubes called the epididymides. While they're traveling, those sperm continue to mature so that they are ready to fertilize an egg to produce a pregnancy (see explanation in Chapter One). They travel through another tube called the vas deferens and make their way through the seminal vesicles. Sperm mix with fluid from the seminal vesicle and the prostate gland, forming semen. When aroused, a guy will pass this semen through the urethra and out the urethral opening. He doesn't really feel all of this going on; he just sees the erection. What's that? Just keep reading.

Erections and Ejaculation

In the hallways at school, an erection is probably called a boner, a hard-on, or, well, a lot of other things that we'd get in trouble for printing. The thing is, there are no bones in the penis, even though it looks that way when the penis is erect. The only thing that makes a penis erect is blood. But let's back up a little bit.

Boys get erections even when they are babies. It is perfectly natural and has nothing to do with interest in

Size Doesn't Matter

Guys cannot help obsessing over their penises. In locker rooms across the nation, boys are looking down and wondering if they measure up. The good news is: You do! For some reason, unusually large penises are associated with masculinity, strength, bravery, and courage. This kind of thinking, no matter how common, is 100-percent nonsense. The size of a guy's penis has nothing to do with his manhood.

A small penis functions just as well as a large one does. Of course, we could repeat ourselves 'til our voice boxes go dead, but that won't stop boys from agonizing about size. Boys want to know what's "normal"—but normal is kind of a dirty word.

Why? Because whether small or large, penises are healthy, natural, and, well, normal (we had to say it!). Still, guys demand statistics. So we'll give them to you as long as you understand that variations above and below the average are common. Here goes: The majority of grown men have a penis that is 3 to 4 inches (8 to 10 centimeters) long when soft. During an erection, the length swells to about 5 to 6 inches (13 to 15 cm) on average.

While we're on our every-penis-is-perfect soap-box, we'll remind you not to listen to myths either. The penises of African American men are the same size as everyone else's. Big feet don't mean big you-know-whats. Long fingers simply mean a guy has long fingers. You get the picture.

sexual activity. Males also tend to have erections in the mornings when they wake up. These are not sexual either. Instead, the bladder, where urine is stored in the body, gets full and triggers nerves at the base of the penis. This causes blood to flow into the shaft and the penis to get hard.

Sexual erections occur at the onset of puberty. A guy may get one from a happy thought or feeling, from his penis being touched or brushed against (even by accident), or from watching a movie or a TV show. It may also happen

Boys get erections even when they are babies. It is perfectly natural and has nothing to do with interest in sexual activity. Males also tend to have erections in the mornings when they wake up.

after he sees someone attractive or from a sexy dream. The regular blood flow that goes in and out of the penis changes just before it becomes erect. Certain muscles allow a lot of blood to come in, while other muscles tighten and keep that blood trapped in the shaft. The spongy walls of the penis expand, and the shaft becomes very stiff. A guy feels pleasurable sensations in the meantime.

If the pleasurable sensations build up enough, he will ejaculate, which means he will release about one teaspoon of semen. (Some kids call this ejaculate "come.") He reaches a peak of excitement at this point, called an orgasm. Ejaculating has the purpose of inserting sperm-rich semen into a woman's vagina. Biologically the sperm are meant to meet her egg and cause a pregnancy. Of course, that's not always what happens. A guy can ejaculate during a dream, when masturbating, or even when he's just making out with someone. After ejaculation, certain muscles relax and allow blood to leave the penis and flow back into the body. Then the shaft becomes soft and spongy once again. It takes only a few minutes for the penis to return to its normal flaccid state.

Wet Dreams

The technical term for a wet dream, when a boy ejaculates during a dream in his sleep, is a nocturnal emission. Wet dreams happen to most guys when puberty starts, around age twelve. They are totally common and sometimes embarrassing for him. But this is his body's way of releasing built-up semen. He may experience them because he is not yet sexually active (which is a good thing if he is not ready!). Masturbating is a healthy way of releasing built-up semen—doing more of it can even curb wet dreams.

Three

The Feelings Frenzy

Growing up involves so much more than just watching your body change. What goes on in your head is far more taxing on you than looking down and seeing pubic hair. What happens when you start feeling romantic about someone? That's probably more difficult to handle.

Your emotional side is maturing right along with your body. Sometimes you'll crave hours and hours of alone time in your room. Other times you may want to spend every second with a close friend. One day you may feel like your parents' mutant alien child because you have nothing in common with them. The following week you may love them more than you ever thought possible. These emotional growing pains go right along with the physical changes. They are a result of your quest for more freedom. It takes a lot of time, tears, and patience to sort things out. The emotional aspects of becoming an adult are as important as what's happening to your body.

A lot of what you're feeling has been linked to hormone levels. They go up and down with no warning during puberty while your body grows and learns to regulate itself, causing a roller coaster of feelings, moodiness, and intensity. Another reasonable explanation for preteen and teen angst is that you're experiencing major events, such as intimate friendship and romantic love, for the first time. Good news: Your up-and-down moods prove you're maturing at the right rate.

Blush, Blush—Crush!

The hormones raging through your body are also responsible for your attraction to other people. Everyone becomes interested in boys or girls at different times. Your best friend may have started developing major crushes in the fourth grade, while you didn't like someone romantically until the eighth grade.

In addition, crushes can vary greatly. One girl may dream of marrying the hot rock star who is on the cover of all the coolest magazines. Another could harbor secret feelings for the cute

English teacher. It's common to have crushes on people you can't really go out with, such as celebrities and authority figures.

Some people will have heterosexual crushes. This means that a person is attracted to members of the opposite sex. Other kids will find they are getting crushes on members of the same sex; they are experiencing homosexual crushes. Still other folks are romantically attracted to members of both sexes, called bisexuality. Just because you have feelings for someone of the same sex doesn't necessarily mean you're bisexual, homosexual, or gay—but it might, and that's okay. If you find yourself having erotic feelings for members of the same sex, you may worry about what your family and friends will say. Luckily, society is more tolerant than ever about homosexuality and bisexuality. Definitely get one-on-one advice from a trusted adult if you have questions about this important topic.

Crushes can be embarrassing because they make you vulnerable. Thirteen-year-old Michelle developed a huge crush on her next-door neighbor when she was eleven. Because he had been a close childhood friend, she was embarrassed to have those feelings. She has kept her crush a secret for two years, with no plans of telling anytime soon.

Whether you share a crush or keep it secret is entirely up to you. Sometimes the fun is in thinking and dreaming about the object of your affection. Others will tell the guys or girls that they like them and see how it goes. This is a gutsy thing to do, but if you're comfortable with it, go for it. One of two things will happen: Your crush will like you back, and you will start hanging out more and talking on the phone. Or your crush won't be interested. Always remember that you didn't do anything wrong if the guy or the girl you like doesn't return the feelings. Sometimes people just don't click. You deserve someone who really likes you for who you are. Never settle for less!

Always remember that you didn't do anything wrong if the guy or the girl you like doesn't return the feelings. Sometimes people just don't click.

The Big Date

You like him; he likes you. So now what? Well, if you're comfortable, and if both sets of parents allow it, you may want to go out with him. That doesn't mean you have to meet up at a posh restaurant and go to a movie afterward. It could mean hanging out together in the hallway between classes or meeting friends at the local pizza place. Talk to your parents about your options. It may seem weird, but your mom or your dad (who has only your best interests in mind) may be able to give you good advice. Or go to someone else you trust. People who are a few years older and have been through it will be happy to help you.

Of course, parents generally make the rules, and they're not the same from one family to the next. Some will let thirteen-year-olds go out on the town; others say that seventeen is too young. There are no steadfast rules on the perfect time to start dating. If you want more freedom, show your family that you are mature and trustworthy. If you have a clean track record—no sneaking out, no getting into trouble at school, good grades—you can remind them that you've made good decisions. They may still say no. In that case, do not yell, explode, or run into your room and slam the door. Those behaviors (tempting as they may be) will only reinforce your parents' belief that you're not yet mature enough to date.

First-Date Tip

It's natural to get nervous before a date—even for people who've been dating for years! We're all nervous for the same reason: We want to be liked. But remember, your date does like you, or you wouldn't be hanging out together!

One way to calm down during a date is to be quiet. Really! When some people are nervous, they tend to talk a lot. Instead of giving in to that temptation, ask your date lots of questions about himself or herself. It's amazing how much more relaxed that little trick can make you both feel.

Yuck! Breaking Up...

Thirteen-year-old Lara had been going out with Steve for a month. As far as she knew, everything was great. "I thought we were so perfect for each other. He had even broken up with his ex to be with me. But Thursday he told me he didn't want to have a girlfriend anymore. On Monday, I heard he spent the entire weekend with his ex. I can't stop crying!"

The down side to dating is heartbreak. There is no other way to put it: It stinks. Everyone gets dumped sometimes. (You will even be the dumper at some point in your life.) While you're getting over a hurt, take a good look at the relationship. Ask yourself, What was good about it? What did you learn? What did you like and dislike about seeing that person? Make each experience worthwhile by learning from it. Then the next one will be that much better.

Despite this, splitting up is painful, and no magic remedy, spell, or curse can cure the hurt. It can take a day, a week, or even a few months before you're okay again. Here are some tips from Dr. Gilda Carle, Ph.D., author of *Teen Talk with Dr. Gilda*, that may make it go a little faster:

1. **Get busy.** If your schedule is packed with worthwhile activities, you don't have time to feel sorry for yourself. So join a club, volunteer, and make lots of plans with friends.

2. **Plan alone time.** Drowning in your tears is a necessary part of the process. If you're feeling bad, lock yourself away for thirty minutes, listen to music, or write in your diary. It's healthy to cry it out. Just set time limits on how long you're allowed to wallow. (When time is up, see step one.)

3. **Get closer.** You will need your friends when you're heartbroken! Depend on them for comfort and companionship. They'll have you feeling better much faster.

When you want to show your parents how grown up you are, calmly negotiate. You may be surprised to find that your parents are willing to compromise. Joy's parents were worried when Charles started calling her, because she was in the seventh grade, and he was in the ninth. To make her parents feel better, Joy asked him to ride his bike to her house and say hello when she knew they were home. "They were really impressed with Charles," Joy says. Although her parents still wouldn't let Joy and Charles go out alone, they did let them go to a restaurant and the movies as long as his older sister went too. "We still have a blast together," she says.

Dating Gone Bad

You already know that taking care of you is your top priority. So don't get caught in a bad relationship. Steer yourself away from a guy or a girl who sets rules, for example. If he doesn't want you to wear a certain outfit or makeup, that's a warning sign that he's too controlling. Jealousy is another thing to watch out for. A good boyfriend or girlfriend will understand when you have friends of the opposite sex. That said, a tiny bit of jealousy is natural and okay. On the other hand, a lot of jealousy—and that means any kind that makes you feel uncomfortable, pressured, or trapped—is very, very bad. A jealous person does not care about you more; he or she simply wants control.

Of course, always stay away from relationships that are physically abusive in any way. If a guy or a girl ever gives you so much as an inappropriate shove, it's time to break up. For help on getting out of an abusive situation, go to the Rape, Abuse, and Incest National Network at *www.rainn.org* for advice. Also, talk to an adult if you or a friend has problems with a relationship.

Dating Gone Good

Wait! We forgot the most important thing: Make sure your date is worthy of you. You can't spend your precious time with someone who isn't a nice, good person, after all. Ask yourself the following questions:

- *Is your date kind and thoughtful of other people? (It's bad news if he or she makes fun in mean ways.)*
- *Does he or she do what they say they'll do (such as call or show up)?*
- *Is he or she concerned about your feelings?*
- *If your family really knew this person, would they like him or her?*
- *Does he or she have a good reputation? (Hopefully, they are not known for two-timing or hurting feelings!)*
- *If you answered even one question "no," think twice about dating this person. You deserve someone who will be considerate and make you happy. Period.*

Let's Get Physical

In our culture, the suggestion of sex is everywhere, all the time. Sex is on television, on roadside advertisements, and in your favorite song lyrics. Yet people still don't feel comfortable discussing the subject. In addition, despite what these messages tell you, sex is not glamorous, nor is it the path to inner happiness. On the other hand, sex is not devilish either. It's a healthy, essential part of being human.

Sex—Explained

"Sexual intercourse is a behavior that has the ability to do the three most powerful things there are, all at the same time," says Deborah Roffman, sex educator and author of *Sex and Sensibility.* "It has the ability to give life, potentially take life away, and to change life forever."

Now that you know all the scientific terms for the male and female anatomy, what exactly are "the birds and the bees?" Reproduction is necessary for each species to continue to thrive on this earth. For humans and many animals, reproduction is a sexual endeavor. In humans, sexual intercourse leads to the continuation of our species. This means that the male inserts his erect penis into the female's vagina. Then he is able to deposit sperm in her body so that at least one of them can bond with an egg and a pregnancy will occur. Of course, sexual intercourse is a pleasurable, intimate, loving activity for human beings, so it is not always done with pregnancy in mind.

> *"Sexual intercourse is a behavior that has the ability to do the three most powerful things there are, all at the same time. It has the ability to give life, potentially take life away, and to change life forever."*

Sex, meaning sexual intercourse, and *sexuality* are often used interchangeably. The truth is, they are totally separate. Sexuality encompasses who you are, how you feel, your desires, interactions, and choices. Sexual interactions—holding hands, kissing, making out, and intercourse—are ways to bring pleasure and express emotions. None of these behaviors are dirty, bad, or wrong. They have a purpose beyond reproduction—to give and receive love, tenderness, warmth, and compassion.

But that doesn't mean a teen who is curious should grab a partner and explore right away! Expressing yourself sexually takes a lot of maturity because it carries many risks, such as an unwanted pregnancy and sexually transmitted diseases (STDs). In addition, showing your sexuality—expressing how your feel—can make you vulnerable to another person, and it can stir up deep emotions. It is a serious endeavor only for people who are 100 percent sure.

Kissing 101

Hopefully, you've found a great partner who is kind, considerate, and worth locking lips with. After you've been hanging around together for a while, you know the big moment—the kiss—is coming. The problem is, you're nervous. Here are some tips to calm jitters:

Hold hands first and flirt to get comfortable before the big smooch. It always boosts your self-confidence to have fresh breath at this point, so make sure those teeth are brushed and you have a mint handy. When things get quiet between the two of you and you find yourselves looking at each other, kissing will come naturally. Wait for that moment and seize it. But if you miss it, no worries. It will happen again.

When you go to kiss someone, part your lips and close your eyes if that makes you feel more comfortable. Once lips meet, do what feels natural. Move them around gently, not too aggressively and not too passively. Pay attention to how your partner is kissing you, and kiss him or her back the same way. Insert your tongue gently, and use it to tease and flirt with your partner's tongue. Practicing isn't so bad.

Doing It—Or Not

"I have been dating my boyfriend for six months, and he really wants to have sex. My body wants to, but I just am not sure if it's the right time for us." —Katie, 14

As a general rule, if you find yourself wondering whether you should go further sexually, you probably shouldn't.

Knowing whether you're ready for more is a common dilemma for both girls and boys. As a general rule, if you find yourself wondering whether you should go further sexually, you probably shouldn't. There is never any harm in waiting. Charles Wibbelsman, M.D., author of *The Teenage Body Book,* suggests that you ask yourself the following questions to help figure it out:

1. **Are you trying to prove something?** Never do something because you feel pressure or because you think everyone else is doing it. You will regret your decision and feel bad about it afterward.

2. **How do you feel about the other person?** Your feelings for each other should be genuine and not about challenge or conquest.

3. **Do you communicate well with your partner?** If you can't talk honestly and openly about sex, feelings, and personal issues with your partner, you are not ready to go further.

4. **Do you know everything there is to know about sex, birth control, pregnancy, and STDs?** This is essential. You must be well educated on all aspects of sex, including its consequences. If you do not know the risks of having sex, you cannot weigh them. See Chapter Five for this important information.

5. Are you ready to deal with the consequences?
What will you do if something major happens as a result of sexual activity? You must know how you will respond in case you get hurt emotionally, wind up pregnant, or contract an STD.

Be patient. Rushing is not necessary. If you take your time and are clear on how you feel, you will make the decision that is right for you.

Oral Sex

In an effort to refrain from intercourse, some teens decide to engage in oral sex, which is when one partner stimulates the other partner's genitals with his or her mouth. A May 2003 Kaiser Foundation study showed that more than one-third of fifteen- to seventeen-year-olds have had oral sex. Half of them do not think it is "as big of a deal as intercourse," while 40 percent believe oral sex is safer.

None of the above beliefs are true. Like intercourse, oral sex is for mature people who can deal with the consequences. The act is just as intimate as intercourse, if not more so, which leaves teens wide open to being taken advantage of emotionally. And while people can't get pregnant from oral sex, they can contract STDs such as herpes, human papilloma virus (HPV), and even HIV (for more information, see Chapter Five).

Twelve Reasons It's Great to Wait

As a pediatrician in California, Dr. Wibbelsman talks with thousands of teens. Here are his reasons to hold off on sex (abstain) from *The Teenage Body Book*:

1. **You are not ready.** Enough said.

2. **Premarital sex goes against your beliefs.** If you compromise what you feel in your gut is right, you will have regrets.

3. **You're in love for the first time.** These incredibly strong new feelings leave you vulnerable to pain and loss. Work on building a strong, nurturing relationship before going to bed together.

4. **You feel pressured.** A partner who truly cares about and values you will not prod you into doing something you're clearly not comfortable with.

Twelve Reasons It's Great to Wait (Continued)

5. **You don't know how to use birth control.** If you have sex without using protection, you'd better get ready to be a parent.

6. **Pregnancy would be disastrous for you.** Even with careful research and the use of birth control, there is still a chance of becoming pregnant. Of course, there is no chance of becoming pregnant if you don't have sex.

7. **You want your first time to be special.** Wait for the right time and the right person to ensure that it will be a pleasurable, memorable, and happy experience.

8. **Your relationship is on the skids.** No problem was ever solved by having sex. If something is wrong in the relationship, adding sexual intercourse to the mix will just complicate matters.

9. **You don't know each other well.** Sexual intercourse is meaningful, pleasurable, an comfortable only with someone who is special to you. Imagine spending an entire day with someone you don't know—sex is ten times more awkward.

10. **You're worried about STDs.** Any time you have sexual intercourse you risk contracting an STD. To stay optimally healthy, abstain.

11. **You don't know much about sex.** Get educated before you think seriously about doing it. You have to know exactly what you're getting into.

12. **You're tempted to have sex for social reasons.** Think it will improve your cool quotient? It won't. Think more people will like you? They might—but not for the right reasons. By having intercourse to be cool or popular, you set yourself up for major disappointments and meaningless, hurtful sexual encounters.

Five

The Sex Consequences

No matter what your age, it's important to be informed about the risks of having sex. Even young married couples often need to think seriously about their ability to handle pregnancy, and everyone should gather all the information he or she can get about sexually transmitted diseases (STDs). Even if you aren't considering sex, you should still know the facts. Get educated on everything sex-related to ensure your safety and solidify the values that work best for you.

"Safe Sex"

According to many experts, the only truly safe sex is no sex at all, called abstinence.

If you don't engage in sexual intercourse or oral sex, the chances of becoming pregnant or getting an STD are zero. Many teens and their parents believe this is the way to go, and they stick to this no-risk strategy.

But facts are facts: According to the 2003 Kaiser Foundation study, one in five people under the age of fifteen have had sexual intercourse. Between the ages of fifteen and seventeen, 37 percent have engaged in sexual intercourse. And according to other studies, 66 percent of young people have had sex by the time they graduate from high school. While abstinence is the only 100-percent safe option, there are ways to practice "safer sex" by using birth control, condoms, and other devices. If you have any questions about birth control, it's important to ask your parents, a guidance counselor, or a health-care provider.

Birth Control

"I am considering sex, but I don't even know the difference between the pill and a diaphragm. I'm way too embarrassed to ask anybody. What should I do?" —Tara, 14

Studies show that up to 20,000 kids in middle school get pregnant every year. That's because they became sexually active without protecting themselves. Pregnancy can occur when a girl who has started menstruating has sexual intercourse with a guy. She can get pregnant any time of the

Pregnancy Happens

The vast majority of teen couples are not prepared for a skipped period and then news of pregnancy. However, this is a real possibility for anyone having sexual intercourse, especially unprotected intercourse. What to do in this case is a highly controversial topic. Your beliefs and moral values will have to guide you.

Having the baby is an option. Even a young girl is physically capable of carrying a baby for nine months until it is born. If a girl decides she wants to have the baby and keep it, she must figure out how she will support it. Almost always, parents must help the teenager.

Adoption is another option. A girl may choose to complete her pregnancy and give the baby to someone else to raise. Many women who make this choice are happy knowing that their child is loved and in a good home. Others find that the pain of being separated from their child is deeper and longer-lasting than they expected.

Abortion is also an option. It is a safe, medically-approved way to end a pregnancy through a surgical procedure or by taking a series of pills. Many people are in favor of abortion as an option; others are very much against it. Both opinions must be respected. For more information about all of these options, go to *www.plannedparenthood.org*.

Studies show that up to 20,000 kids in middle school get pregnant every year. That's because they became sexually active without protecting themselves.

month because a female at any age can never be totally sure when she will ovulate. It doesn't matter if he pulls out before ejaculating or not. Birth control gives people of all ages reliable—though not foolproof—options for preventing pregnancies. Through use of many modern products, couples can choose *not* to have children even though they are engaging in sexual intercourse. See the chart on pp. 69–72 for a list of the different types of birth control.

Sexually Transmitted Diseases

STDs are infections that occur after sexual interaction. They are passed from one person to another during sexual intercourse, anal intercourse, and even oral sex. Some are very serious and even life threatening (such as HIV), while others are easily treatable.

The only way to be 100-percent protected is to abstain from sex. Otherwise, prevention methods—such as condoms and spermicides—should be used to minimize the risk of getting an STD. Don't be embarrassed if you see something unusual "down there." Just seek treatment ASAP.

Bacterial Vaginosis

What it is: Sometimes sexual intercourse can disrupt the bacterial balance in the vagina, and harmful bacteria can take over. (BV is not always sexually transmitted, by the way.) Only women can get BV.

Symptoms: Unpleasant vaginal odor and grayish discharge.

How you get it: From taking antibiotics or vaginal intercourse.

How to prevent it: Condoms offer good protection.

How to cure it: See a doctor for prescription medicine.

Chlamydia

What it is: One in ten teens gets infected with chlamydia, an infection caused by a bacterium.

Symptoms: Discharge from the penis or the vagina, pain or burning when urinating, painful intercourse in women. Many people have no symptoms, so if you're sexually active it's important to tell your physician—most doctors automatically screen for this common STD, which can cause infertility.

How you get it: From vaginal or anal intercourse.

How to prevent it: Condoms offer good protection.

How to cure it: Both partners must take prescription antibiotics.

Genital Herpes

What it is: A virus that causes painful sores or warts on the genitals, it is related to the virus that causes sores in the mouth.

Symptoms: Tiny clusters of painful blisters on the anus, the vulva, or the penis.

How you get it: From vaginal or anal intercourse, oral sex, or other contact with blisters. (*Note, it is possible to get infected when someone with oral herpes performs oral sex on a partner.)

How to prevent it: Condom use helps.

How to cure it: Herpes isn't curable, but outbreaks can be minimized with drug therapies.

Human Papilloma Virus (HPV)

What it is: There are more than sixty types of HPVs, and nearly three-fourths of Americans have one form or another. HPVs can cause a variety of genital warts, though sometimes they have no symptoms at all. Sometimes they cause cancer of the cervix or of the penis.

Symptoms: None, or warts on the genitals and the anus. Blisters may be in clusters and can become itchy.

How you get it: From vaginal or anal intercourse or oral sex.

How to prevent it: Condom use helps.

How to cure it: HPV isn't curable, but outbreaks can be minimized with proper treatment.

Gonorrhea

What it is: Gonorrhea is caused by a bacterium that can cause sterility, arthritis, and heart problems.

Symptoms: Painful urination, genital discharge, vaginal or pelvic pain; sometimes, there are no symptoms at all.

How you get it: From vaginal or anal intercourse or oral sex.

How to prevent it: Condoms are very effective.

How to cure it: Both partners must be treated with oral antibiotics. Often people with gonorrhea also have chlamydia. They must be treated for both infections at the same time.

Pubic lice

What they are: Parasites that lay eggs in the pubic hair.

Symptoms: Intense itching.

How you get it: Sexual contact.

How to prevent it: Limit the number of sexual partners and contacts.

How to cure it: Prescription topical ointment or a nonprescription drug called A-2000; clothing and bedding must be disinfected.

Scabies

What it is: A mite that burrows under the skin.

Symptoms: Intense itching on the penis, the fingers, the buttocks, the breasts, the wrists, the thighs, or the navel.

How you get it: Close personal contact.

How to prevent it: Limit the number of sexual partners and contacts.

HIV and AIDS

HIV, the human immunodeficiency virus, is by far the scariest, deadliest STD of our time. HIV works by breaking down a person's immune system, which means the body cannot fight back when it is sick. As a result, someone who is HIV-positive will contract many, many illnesses. HIV is often silent, with no major symptoms for up to ten years after a person has been infected. Usually an infected man or woman will experience a slight fever, headaches, fatigue, muscle aches, and swollen glands in the first stages of this devastating disease. AIDS, short for Acquired Immune Deficiency Syndrome, is the most advanced stage of HIV and the deadliest.

Up to 25 percent of all new HIV infections occur in people ages thirteen to twenty-one. The vast majority of new infections in teenagers are the result of un-protected vaginal intercourse. But that is not the only way to contract this disease. In addition to being transmitted in semen and vaginal fluids, HIV is also passed along in breast milk and blood (for instance, by sharing needles with an infected person or getting HIV-infected blood into an open wound or sore). In past decades, HIV could be spread through blood transfusions, but because of today's much-improved screening processes this is so rare that it shouldn't worry you.

Just as you need to know how HIV is transmitted, it's very important to understand the ways that HIV is *not* spread from one person to another. It cannot be passed along by casual contact such as kissing, sharing water glasses, or hugging. You also cannot get it from donating blood.

The only way to be absolutely sure you never contract the disease is to abstain from vaginal and anal intercourse, drug use, and oral sex. If you decide to have sex, be as safe as possible. Correct condom use offers excellent—but not 100-percent—protection against the disease. If you suspect you have HIV, the only way to find out for sure is to get a blood test from a doctor or a health clinic. You can also buy a home health-test kit at most drugstores. For additional information and guidance, talk to the school nurse or contact the National AIDS hotline at 800-342-AIDS.

Although there is no cure for HIV or AIDS, those with HIV can receive treatments that will improve and prolong their lives. In rare cases, some people who are HIV-positive never develop AIDS. Scientists are studying these people in the hopes of finding a cure.

How to cure it: Topical prescription treatment and disinfection of clothing and bedding.

Syphilis

What it is: Syphilis is caused by a bacterium that can cause disfigurement, neurological disorder, or death.

Symptoms: Painless sores on the genitals, the rectum, the lips, or the mouth followed by a rash, swollen joints, and flulike illness.

How you get it: From vaginal and anal intercourse and oral sex.

How to prevent it: Condom use is very effective.

How to cure it: Antibiotics for both partners, but damage caused by the disease in its later phases cannot be undone.

Trichomoniasis

What it is: Caused by a protozoan—a microscopic, one-cell animal—"trich" is a common cause of vaginal infections.

Symptoms: For females, frothy, greenish yellow vaginal discharge; inflammation of the vulva; frequent and painful urination; or itching. Males rarely have symptoms.

How you get it: Vaginal intercourse.

How to prevent it: Condom use is very effective.

How to cure it: Antibiotics for both partners.

Birth Control: The Facts

Form of Birth Control	Protection Against STDs	Effectiveness*

When used exactly according to the directions!

Form of Birth Control	Protection Against STDs	Effectiveness*
<u>Condoms</u> A condom is a thin sheath of latex, plastic, or sheepskin that is worn over the penis during sexual intercourse. It prevents semen from entering the vagina. Latex and plastic condoms are 98 percent effective when used according to the directions. Sheepskin condoms are less effective.	Yes	98 percent
<u>Female condoms</u> This thin sheath of polyurethane is inserted into the vagina. One end goes over the cervix, the shaft of the female condom protects the vaginal canal, and the other end opens up to allow the penis to enter. It prevents semen from entering the vagina. Female condoms are available over the counter.	Yes	80 percent

Form of Birth Control	Protection Against STDs	Effectiveness
<u>Oral contraceptives/birth control pills</u> Made of combinations of hormones, these prescription-only pills prevent the ovaries from releasing an egg each month. They also work by changing the quality of the lining of the uterus so that a fertilized egg would have difficulty attaching to it. Pills are taken every day of the twenty-eight day menstrual cycle, and a female still has her period as usual.	No	99 percent
<u>Injections</u> New drugs such as Depo-Provera can be injected either once a month or once every three months to prevent pregnancy. The shots work much like the pill. A health care provider must give this prescription and the shot.	No	99 percent

The ring This small, flexible ring is inserted into the vagina for three weeks and taken out for the fourth week. It releases synthetic hormones to protect against pregnancy for one month. Available by prescription only.	No	99 percent
The patch This thin, beige, plastic patch is applied to the skin of the buttocks, the stomach, the upper outer arm, or the upper torso once a week for three out of four weeks. It releases synthetic hormones to protect against pregnancy. Available by prescription only.	No	99 percent
Diaphragms/cervical caps These are shallow, cone-shape cups. Before intercourse, one diaphragm or cap is inserted into the vagina, where it fits over the cervix to prevent semen from fertilizing an egg. Spermicides must be put into the diaphragm or cap before insertion. A health-care provider must fit the female with the diaphragm or cervical cap to be sure it is the right size.	No	97 percent

Birth Control: The Facts (Continued)

Form of Birth Control	Protection Against STDs	Effectiveness
Spermicides Available as a jelly, a cream, a foam, a film (an opaque sheet you can insert), or suppository, spermicides kill sperm through the use of chemicals. They are more effective when used with condoms, diaphragms, or cervical caps. Spermicides are available over the counter.	No	70 percent *(alone)*
Morning-after pills/emergency contraception (EC) This series of pills can prevent fertilization or, when taken 72 hours after unprotected intercourse, implantation after unprotected vaginal intercourse. You can request EC if you think your contraceptive method has failed, or if you've been forced to have unprotected sex. To receive the pills, you need to see your physician.	No	89-95 percent *(when taken 72 hours after unprotected intercourse)*

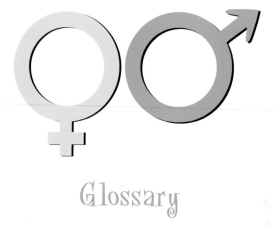

Glossary

abstinence: the act of refraining from sexual intercourse

AIDS: Acquired Immune Deficiency Syndrome, this is a breakdown of the body's immune system due to HIV

arousal: when a person becomes sexually excited

birth control: methods of avoiding pregnancy that include taking pills, using condoms, and abstinence

cervix: muscular structure at the end of the vaginal canal that acts as the neck of the uterus; the cervix allows sperm into the uterus for fertilization, and it expands during childbirth

clitoris: a pea-size bit of flesh in the female body with the sole purpose of making its owner feel good during sexual arousal estrogen: a hormone found in greater quantities in the female body; when the pituitary glands begin making more estrogen in girls, puberty begins

heterosexual: a person who is romantically and sexually attracted to people of the opposite sex

HIV: Human Immunodeficiency Virus, a retrovirus that causes AIDS by infecting the immune system

homosexual: a person who is romantically and sexually attracted to people of the same sex

hymen: a thin ring of tissue located just outside the vaginal opening; it can expand and even tear ("break") during tampon insertion or vigorous activity such as horseback riding or sexual intercourse

menstrual cycle: a female reproductive process involving ovulation, changes in the tissue lining of the uterus, and the shedding of that lining through menstrual blood flow

penis: the male reproductive organ that fills with blood and becomes rigid during sexual arousal; the organ also allows urine to exit the body

puberty: the process of physically becoming an adult, which typically begins when a person is eight to nine years old and ends at around age eighteen sexual intercourse: the act of human reproduction in which the male inserts his penis into the female vagina; the act can also produce immense pleasure

sexuality: the part of oneself that is expressed sexually; the condition of being characterized and distinguished by sex

STDs: sexually transmitted diseases, these are infections and diseases that humans get due to sexual activity; some STDs, such as HIV, are extremely dangerous

testicles: the ball-shaped organs located inside the scrotum; they are also called testes (commonly referred to as "balls") and serve as the centers for sperm cells and testosterone production in males

testosterone: a hormone found in greater quantities in the male body

uterus: the small, muscular, pear-shape structure that holds a baby during pregnancy; the uterus builds and sheds its lining approximately once a month during the menstrual cycle

vagina: the canal that leads from the opening of the vulva to the cervix of the uterus; the vagina is also the passage for menstrual and other discharges

Further Resources

Books

Carle, Gilda, Ph.D. *Teen Talk with Dr. Gilda: A Girl's Guide to Dating.* New York, NY: Quill, 2003.

Drill, Esther, Heather McDonald, and Rebecca Odes. *Deal with It! A Whole New Approach to Your Body, Brain, and Life as a Gurl.* New York, NY: Pocket Books, 1999.

Gravelle, Karen. *What's Going On Down There? Answers to Questions Boys Find Hard to Ask.* New York, NY: Walker & Company, 1998.

Wibbelsman, Charles, M.D. *The Teenage Body Book.* New York, NY: The Berkeley Publishing Group, 1999.

Online Sites and Organizations

Go Ask Alice!
www.goaskalice.columbia.edu
A University of Michigan study published in the December 2000 *Health Education & Behavior* journal names Go Ask Alice! number one for access to specific sexual health information on the Internet. It is produced by the health professionals at Columbia University in New York City.

National Coalition for Gay, Lesbian, Bisexual, &
Transgender Youth
369 Third Street, Suite B-362
San Rafael, CA 94901-3581
www.outproud.org
Resources and information for alternative youth lifestyles.

National STD Hotline
(800) 227-8922
www.ashastd.org/NSTD
This Web site can answer all of your questions about STDs and
tell you where to find help in your hometown.

TeensHealth
www.teenhealth.org/teen
TeensHealth was created for teens looking for honest, accurate
information and advice about health, relationships, and growing
up. Created by The Nemours Foundation's Center for Children's
Health Media, TeensHealth and KidsHealth have been providing
teens and families with accurate, up-to-date, and jargon-free
health information since 1995.

Teenwire
www.teenwire.com
This site by Planned Parenthood is the teen arm of the organization and specifically deals with your questions about sexuality.

Index

About the Author

Kristen Kemp is the author of *The Dating Diaries* (Scholastic, 2004), and five other young-adult novels. She has written eight other non-fiction books, including *Vulvodynia: A Survivor's Guide*. She also writes features for national and local publications such as *CosmoGirl!*, *Girls' Life, Glamour, Ladies' Home Journal, Marie Claire*, and the *New York Daily News*. She is currently the GL Body columnist at *Girls' Life* and was formerly the writer of *YM's* Ask Anything column.

Kristen teaches young-adult novel writing to New Yorkers through a professional organization for journalists in New York City. She lives with her boyfriend, cat, and dog just north of Scholastic's Manhattan headquarters.

Acknowledgements

My deepest appreciation to Cathryn Tobin, M.D., author of The Parent's Problem Solver, *a pediatrician, licensed midwife, and a member of the Canadian Pediatrics Society and the Royal College of Physicians and Surgeons in Ontario, Canada, for her guidance and expertise.*

Special thanks to Charles Wibbelsman, M.D., author of The Teenage Body Book, *chairman of the chiefs of adolescent medicine for the Permanente Medical Group of Northern California, chief of the Teenage Clinic at Kaiser Permanente and associate professor of pediatrics at the University of California, San Francisco, Medical School, who has offered excellent advice for this book and for many of my teen magazine assignments.*